Cubes

ABC

BY NANCY FURSTINGER

Published by The Child's World®
1980 Lookout Drive • Mankato, MN 56003-1705
800-599-READ • www.childsworld.com

Acknowledgments
The Child's World®: Mary Berendes, Publishing Director
Red Line Editorial: Editorial direction
The Design Lab: Design

Photographs ©: Shutterstock Images, cover (bottom
right), 1 (bottom right), 4, 5, 13, 20, 22; Valdis Torms/
Shutterstock Images, cover (top left), 1 (top left),
3 (left), 9; Jakub Krechowicz/Shutterstock Images,
cover (top right), 1 (top right), 3 (right); Thinkstock,
cover (bottom left), 1 (bottom left), 14; Dmitri
Maruta/Shutterstock Images, 6; Wave Break
Media/Shutterstock Images, 10; Africa Studio/
Shutterstock Images, 12; Polka Dot/Thinkstock, 15;
Ingram Publishing/Thinkstock, 16; Surkov Vladimir/
Shutterstock Images, 17; Vaclav Taus/Shutterstock
Images, 18; Valentyn Volkov/Shutterstock Images, 21

ISBN 9781623239824
LCCN 2013947241

Printed in the United States of America
Mankato, MN
November, 2013
PA02194

ABOUT THE AUTHOR

Award-winning author Nancy
Furstinger enjoys searching
for inspiring shapes in nature
as she hikes with her big
pooches. She is the author of
more than 100 books.

CONTENTS

ROLLING THE DICE

You're playing a board game with your friends. You roll two dice. You call out the numbers as you move your game piece forward. One! Two! Three! Four! Will you get to roll again, or will you lose a turn?

Rolling dice in many board games tells you how far to move your game piece.

While you're waiting for your next turn, you add some ice to your lemonade. Did you notice how the shape of the dice matches the shape of the ice? Both of these shapes are **cubes**.

Ice in cubes can cool your drink.

There are many wooden blocks in this picture. How many cubes can you count?

WHAT DOES A CUBE LOOK LIKE?

You can find cube shapes everywhere. Cubes have three **dimensions**. They aren't flat. Flat shapes, like a square, have only two dimensions: length and width. Other names for these flat shapes are plane shapes or 2-D shapes.

We can measure all three dimensions of a cube: length, width, and height. Shapes with three dimensions are called **3-D** shapes. Another name for 3-D shapes is solid shapes.

How do we know a shape is a cube? Look closely. A cube has six square **faces**. Each of the six faces is exactly equal in size. Like a square, the lengths and widths of each face are the same. These faces are 2-D flat **surfaces**. Each face forms a surface of a 3-D shape.

A cube has 12 **edges** where two faces come together. A cube also has eight **corners**.

Another word for the corner of a shape is a **vertex**. A cube has eight vertices.

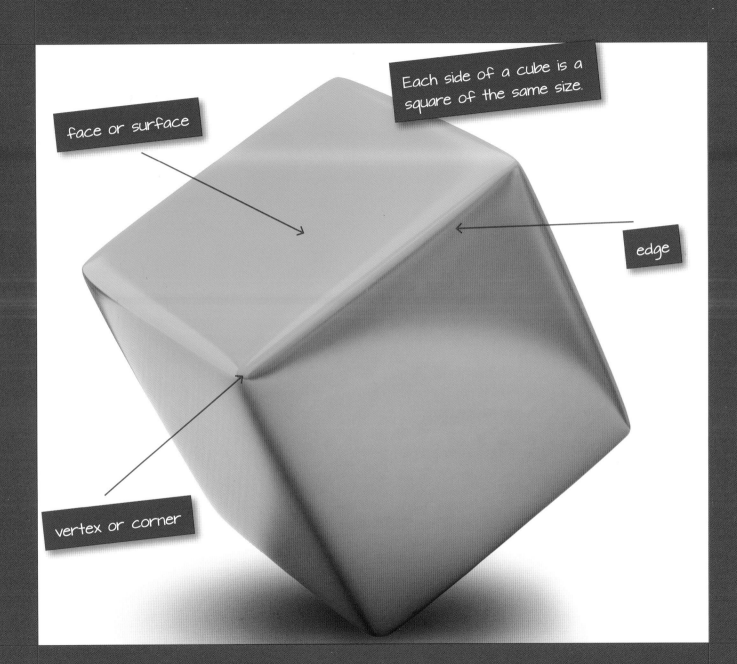

face or surface

Each side of a cube is a square of the same size.

edge

vertex or corner

9

STACKING UP CUBES

Now you know what a cube looks like. Keep looking, and you'll find this 3-D shape all around you.

You can build all kinds of things with cube-shaped blocks.

Your little sister is learning to read. She plays with a set of 26 alphabet blocks. Each cube-shaped block has a letter of the alphabet stamped on one of its six faces. The other five faces show pictures of things that begin with that letter.

Stack the blocks to make a bigger cube—four blocks make a square on the bottom layer with four more on top.

Your sister has fun stacking the blocks and knocking them down. Then it's time to clean up. You help her put the blocks inside a toy chest. The toy chest has six square faces of equal size. It is also a cube.

Playing with the Alphabet

For hundreds of years, children have been learning how to read by playing with alphabet blocks. These homemade blocks help toddlers recognize the shapes of letters. Alphabet blocks are still popular today. This classic toy in now in the National Toy Hall of Fame!

SNACKING ON CUBES

Cubes make a handy shape for
snacking. Your mother brings
you a tray of tasty snacks. She
has all of your favorite foods
cut up into cubes.

We make frozen cubes
using an ice-cube tray.
Frozen chocolate ice cubes
dress up a glass of milk. Frozen
fruit juice cubes jazz up drinks.

When we freeze a wooden stick in a pudding cube, we will soon have a tasty popsicle!

We also toss sugar cubes into pitchers of lemonade. These small cubes are handy for making drinks sweet. A tool called a sugar cube press was invented in the 1800s.

Sometimes candy comes in cubes. Can you think of other cube-shaped foods?

SURPRISES IN CUBES

It's moving day! We fill cube-shaped boxes of all sizes. Big boxes hold toys. Medium boxes hold clothes. Small boxes hold books. Remember to label all of those boxes! Maybe your new bedroom will be shaped like a cube, too.

Boxes can hold many surprises. What types of presents might come in cube-shaped boxes?

Have you ever helped pack boxes? What did you pack up?

The Rubik's Cube puzzle can be difficult to solve.

Rubik's Cube

One of the most famous cubes ever is the Rubik's Cube. Emo Rubik invented this 3-D puzzle in 1974. To solve it, people twist the cube until the nine small squares on each face are the same color. The world record to solve the puzzle is a speedy 5.55 seconds! People around the world have bought more than 300 million cubes. These cubes could stretch from the North Pole to the South Pole!

CUBES AROUND THE HOUSE

A cube aquarium makes a great home for pets. A bright blue beta fish shares the tank with an African dwarf frog. The two friends swim back and forth. They lounge in lush green water plants. They nibble on pellets and fish food flakes.

The oldest pet goldfish lived 25 years!

Far below the tank, your pet dog plays with a cube-shaped toy. Sit down and relax as you put your feet up on a cube-shaped footrest. Up on the bookshelf, a cube holds up a row of books. There's a photo cube there, too. Each side has a different family snapshot.

Are any of your toys shaped like cubes? What cubes can you find in your house?

CUBES IN ART

Did you know that there was an art movement inspired by 3-D shapes? Cubism started in France in the early 1900s. Artists painted figures made up of different shapes, including cubes. They wanted to show a

A Cubist painting looks at how we draw 2-D flat shapes to look like 3-D solids.

3-D figure on a flat 2-D surface. The art they created looked like it had been cut apart and then glued back together.

Pablo Picasso

Pablo Picasso was a cofounder of the Cubist movement. This Spanish artist took apart familiar figures and studied their shapes. He painted portraits that showed all the sides of a face from different angles. Many of the pictures were painted in cool blues and warm browns. He wanted people to see the shape of the figure and how it was put together instead of color.

CUBES IN NATURE

If you want to find cube shapes in nature, bring a magnifying glass. Crystals are a type of rock. Some tiny crystals are cube-shaped.

Another rock called pyrite is sometimes shaped like a cube. You might know pyrite by a different name: fool's gold. This shiny golden mineral is only rich in color!

Farmers in Japan created cube-shaped watermelons. They're easier to ship and

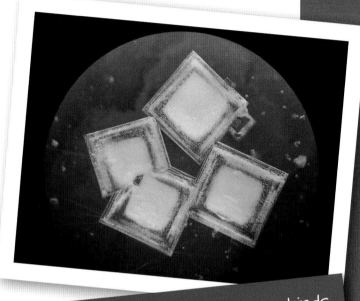

Salt is a crystal. Some kinds of salt crystals look like cubes under a microscope.

stack at markets than the usual round melons. And they won't roll out of your refrigerator! How are these watermelons formed? As the baby watermelon grows on a vine, the farmer places a glass cube around the fruit. Then the watermelon fills that shape as it ripens. If you want one of these watermelons, save your allowance. Each one costs 10,000 yen, or about $83.

Now farmers in the United Arab Emirates grow these melon cubes. They also grow cubed tomatoes and cucumbers.

Look for cube shapes everywhere you go. You might be surprised how many of these 3-D shapes you can find!

HANDS-ON ACTIVITY: CUBE SCAVENGER HUNT

Search for cube shapes in your school. Describe what you find in your notebook and where you discovered it, then tally up your score!

Materials

- small notebook
- pencil
- watch

Directions

1. Divide into teams.
2. Match up your watches. Agree to meet back in your classroom in a half hour.
3. Explore your school to discover as many cube-shaped objects as possible.
4. Don't forget to record the name of the cube and where your team found it.
5. Return to your classroom and count up all of the cubes you discovered. Which team found the most?

GLOSSARY

corners (KOR-nurs): Corners are the points or places where edges or sides meet. Cubes have eight corners.

cubes (KYOOBS): Cubes are 3-D shapes with six equal, square sides. Dice and alphabet blocks are two examples of cubes.

dimensions (duh-MEN-shuns): Dimensions are the length, width, or height of an object. A cube's height is one of its dimensions.

edges (EJ-uhs): Edges are the lines where a surface begins or ends. A cube's edges are where each square face meets.

faces (FASE-uhs): Faces are flat surfaces on a 3-D shape. A cube has six square faces.

surfaces (SUR-fas-uhs): Surfaces are the flat or curved borders of a 3-D shape. A cube has six square surfaces.

3-D (THREE-DEE): A 3-D shape has three dimensions, length, width, and height. A 3-D shape is not flat.

vertex (VUR-teks): A vertex is the point where the edges of a 3-D shape meet. The vertex on a cube is where three square faces meet. A cube has eight vertices.

BOOKS

Cohen, Marina. *My Path to Math: 3-D Shapes*. New York: Crabtree
Publishing Company, 2011.
Hoban, Tana. *Cubes, Cones, Cylinders, & Spheres*. New York: Greenwillow
Books, 2000.

WEB SITES

Visit our Web site for links about Cubes: *childsworld.com/links*

Note to Parents, Teachers, and Librarians:
We routinely verify our Web links to make sure they are safe and active sites.
So encourage your readers to check them out!

INDEX